Walking Through The Darkness

by
Jeff Warner

PRESS

This book is first dedicated to Jesus Christ,
my great Sustainer.

This book is further dedicated to
my wonderful children,
Jimmy, Danny, Katie and Johnny
who continue to teach me how to come
to Jesus as a child.

Table of Contents

The people who walk in darkness
will see a great light;
Those who live in a dark land,
the light will shine on them.
Isaiah 9:2

"I am the Light of the world;
he who follows Me will not walk in the darkness,
but will have the Light of life."
John 8:12

Preface

I believe this book is a gift from God to me and I want to share it with you. My life, like yours, has been filled with pain. What do you do when God is silent? What do you do when you feel invisible? What do you do when circumstances seem to continually give you the short end of the stick? What do you do when misunderstandings and injustices seem to abound? Where is God in the dark times of life?

While wrestling through these issues and others, God began to open my eyes to see a part of Him that I had never seen before. This illumination was life-giving and revolutionary!

Contained in these pages are eternal truths I believe God wants shared with a hurting world. These truths say that there is value in suffering and in enduring. Through these truths you can encounter God in a personal way that allows His peace to permeate your heart while in the midst of some of life's most challenging circumstances.

Although I do not give details of my personal journey, this book is autobiographical of the faith journey I have walked, of the faith journey of others who've walked before me and the faith journey of many others who are yet to follow.

My prayer is that you too may encounter the living God in a very real and personal way as you walk through your darkness.

Entering the Darkness

"In the world you have tribulation,
but take courage; I have overcome the world."
John 16:33

Pain. It seems like life is filled with pain. Some pain is a consequence of mistakes you've made-things you've done or things you should have done. In some respects, pain from choices you make seems relatively easier to accept since it's more clearly tied to an action or inaction over which you had more control.

What about pain that is inflicted upon you through no fault of your own? What if you've been sexually assaulted? Grown up in an abusive home? Been harmed by those who should have protected you? Suffered for doing right? Been physically impaired from an accident caused by someone else? Betrayed by a friend? Been cheated by a friend or business partner? What about friends and family who've been hurt or killed as a result of someone else's negligence?

Sometimes it feels like you're just walking in the darkness. You're lost. You're surrounded by chaos.

You have no idea which way to go. It feels like your world is closing in upon you. It's just frightening, terrifying and even paralyzing.

How do these experiences line up with the goodness of God? How do these fit with God being all-powerful? Would a loving God really allow these events to happen?

Your answer to these questions will greatly affect your life. Will you move closer to God, surrender control to Him and experience Him in the darkness and confusion? Or will you push God aside and take control of your life and keep God at a distance, fueled by the apparent abandonment and betrayal you've experienced from Him?

A few years ago, I wrestled with these questions. In fact, they brought me to a crisis of faith. I greatly questioned and grappled with the goodness, love, power and control of God. Without more clarity, I was seriously questioning not only the goodness of God, but also His very existence.

This is a difficult position for anyone to be in, yet I was in a unique position...I'm a pastor! How can I lead the people of God when I'm questioning His very existence?

Some will argue that when bad things happen to good people it is because this domain, the earth, belongs to satan. I would submit that satan has never been given a license to operate outside the will of God. As a created being, satan has been and continues to be under the control and power of God. He is unable to operate outside the expressed consent and will of God.

The implications of this are enormous. Although you may not know if God or satan ordained the terrible events of your life, you can be certain that if God is in charge, then God "allowed" or "permitted" these terrible events to happen. Let me say that again - God allowed or permitted these terrible events to happen! Permitting is not the same as causing. For some of you, this is almost an unimaginable statement. Did God allow your rape? Did God allow your abuse? Did God allow the accident that has forever changed your life? Did God allow your friend to betray you? Did God allow you to be cheated? Did God allow that untimely death? I would submit that the radical answer is a resounding and confident "yes!" This harsh reality began to greatly disturb me as I sense it may disturb you as well.

As I began to seek God, my eyes were opened to some common verses I had known for years. As I share them with you, please do not allow their familiarity to cause you to dismiss them or to quickly pass over them. Their truths are deep and profound and after over 10 years of knowing them, God took me deeper into these verses. I hope He will do the same with you.

John 3:16 (NIV) "For God so loved the world that He gave His one and only Son, that whoever believes in Him shall not perish but have eternal life."

This verse is the most translated and most well known verse around the globe. Yet its truth somehow landed in my head and missed its place in my heart.

As I prayed over this verse, I was gripped by God and His perfections: His perfect love; His perfect presence in all places at all times; His perfect power; His perfect knowledge and His perfect justice.

During my reflection upon God, I was drawn to His love. His unrelenting, selfless, sacrificial love hunted me down and was so overwhelming that it led me to repentance. God didn't love me from the leftovers of His abundance or affluence; God loved me from His sacrificial love, the love that gave me and you the best through His begotten Son, Jesus.

It's often easier for me to think of God loving the world. Yet, as I meditated on this verse, it was as if God said, "Jeff, you're part of the world. Why don't you put your name here?" I was a bit dumbfounded and embarrassed. The words felt surprisingly awkward..."For God so loved <u>Jeff</u>..." You could plug your name in there as well. "For God so loved _____."

I was stunned and taken back. I realized that my service to God was more motivated by my sense of duty and responsibility than by my love for Him. I believed God loved me for what I did for Him, not for who I was. My heart was revealed. I believed the age-old lie; I felt I needed to earn God's love. Somehow, I felt I didn't deserve it, and truthfully I did not. However, although I didn't deserve God's love and forgiveness, He gave it to me because He loves and values me. He wanted a relationship with me.

The experience was refreshing. God loves me! He loves me and He died for me to be in a relationship eternally with Him. That's love!

Friends, God loves me and He loves you. That's a truth that will change the world and that's why it's called "Good News!"

There's more:

Romans 5:8 (NIV) "But God demonstrates His own love for us in this: While we were still sinners, Christ died for us."

God doesn't just talk about His love; He proves it. He demonstrates it. That's what the cross and empty tomb are all about. In that place where I was in rebellion to God, shaking my fist at Him and turning my back on Him, in that very place, God reached down from Heaven, He lived, He died and He rose from the dead out of His love and desire for me. His desire and hope was that I would respond to His love so that we would experience an eternity together. That was powerful!

Romans 8:32 (NIV) "He who did not spare His own Son, but gave Him up for us all-how will He not also along with Him, graciously give us all things?"

God has given me the very best. It only made sense that if I was that special and had gotten the best already, seeing God's commitment toward me, wouldn't He give me the other less essential things I needed?

Romans 8:29 (NIV) "For those God foreknew, He also predestined to become conformed to the likeness of His Son."

God's desire and commitment to me and to you is for us to be like Jesus. That will be true for sure in Heaven, yet it is His desire for us here on earth as well.

Even the Apostle Paul says in Philippians 1:6 that God will complete His work in you until the day of Christ Jesus. God is going to keep working on me and on you until the return of Jesus. The clear implication is that He is working now and will continue His work until He returns.

In these verses, I was challenged with the undeniable historical truth of Jesus' life, death and resurrection…for me and for the world.

These truths pierced my heart. Without them, how could I begin to understand the pain in my life? If God doesn't care or is busy or is silent, why should I trust or believe in such a wretched God? But if God is as loving and good as He says, there must be some higher purpose in my suffering. Could I somehow look at the circumstances of my life through the lens of an almighty and all loving God?

As I began to seek God, I was struck by the unbelievable circumstances that God allowed some of His faithful servants to experience.

If you have never surrendered your life to God through Jesus, please read "Encountering God" located in the Appendix.

Below are true stories of men and woman who were challenged in ways perhaps far greater than you or me. I challenge you to put yourself in their situation. Seek to experience the unbelievable journey of faith to which God called them.

Story 1–Matt

Consider "Matt," a man who loved God. Matt had a godly wife and family. He sought to glorify God through his business, family and life. Then through no fault of his own, all of his children were killed and a short time later, his business went belly up.

In the midst of this enormous emotional and spiritual challenge, Matt was stricken with a very painful illness where even the slightest touch brought excruciating pain. He genuinely sought to understand why God would let this happen to him, but God did not seem to answer.

In his quest to make sense of this seemingly senseless situation, Matt went to his closest friends for comfort. Instead of support and love, he is met with suspicion and doubt, not quite the response he hoped for. His struggle lasted for several years of his life!

Matt felt powerless, lost, hopeless and misunderstood. What would you think about God in this circumstance? What kind of God could be so silent during a time of such need?

Story 2 – Kwamee & Latisha

"Kwamee & Latisha" loved God. They gave their lives for His service. They were very much in love with each other and greatly desired a family, yet they were unable to bear children. Finally their worst fear was confirmed; they were infertile! The years passed and they continued to serve God… childless.

Imagine if your closest friends came up and shared with you that "God has told me you're going to have a child." This happened to Kwamee & Latisha. For them and other couples like them, such a thing would seem to be a cruel joke, not very funny and extremely hurtful. It would be like pouring salt in an open wound. They struggled with this issue for most of their lives!

Kwamee & Latisha felt abandoned, cheated and neglected by the very God who is the Creator. The very God who spoke the universe into existence didn't/wouldn't give them children.

Those of you who have experienced this struggle or know of a couple that has wrestled with infertility understand in part the agony and despair that this situation brings. What would you do? How would you respond?

Story 3–Angie

"Angie" was one of the most beautiful and talented women in town. Her future was bright and hopeful and she longed to marry, settle down and raise a family. Then one fateful day she was kidnapped and made a love slave for a very selfish and powerful man. With her dreams dashed and her future destroyed, she spent the remainder of her life under his control!

Angie wrestled with being powerless, gripped by fear and loneliness. How could God have abandoned her? How could He have allowed such a terrible atrocity to occur to such a beautiful and faithful follower?

What would you think about a God who would allow this to happen? How would you respond? What if Angie was your daughter? Could you share with her that God allowed this for good according to His perfect will?

Story 4 – Kyle

"Kyle" was a young, proud boy, yet very passionate about God. One night, he sensed God speaking to Him in a dream, calling him to a powerful ministry that would have far-reaching effects. His family, although God-fearing, doubted his encounter and reproved him for his arrogance. Over time and through a series of unusual events, he was unjustly thrown into prison. Even though completely innocent, Kyle lost about 13 years of his life because of this injustice!

Who can imagine the pain, confusion, doubt, betrayal, abandonment and injustice with which Kyle must have wrestled? Where was his God? What about his dream? Did he just imagine it or did he really hear from God? How would you respond to this significant loss?

Story 5 – Ed

"Ed" was a faithful boy. His tasks were menial and mundane...yet he loved God and viewed his jobs as an act of worship before God and God blessed him. In the course of time, Ed was notified that he had been selected to be the next in line for a prominent position. As time went by, Ed came to deeply respect the man he would eventually replace and the man respected Ed – for a time. As time went by, Ed's mentor became increasingly jealous of Ed and the opportunity Ed would get, especially considering Ed's young age. Ed's mentor even plotted to have him assassinated!

Ed continued to trust God, and even though he had opportunity to take the life of his boss in self-defense, he did not. He had entrusted his situation to God.

For almost 15 years, Ed's life plans were on hold due to the insecurity and evil of his mentor. He had to move far away from his family and his friends and even go into hiding.

Ed grappled with betrayal, disappointment, abandonment, injustice and inequity.

Where was his loving God? Why would God allow such an evil man to triumph over such a righteous, godly young man? What happened to the justice and fairness of God?

Story 6 – Tim & Denise

"Tim & Denise" were so in love. They were young, but mature for their age. Their families were excited and supportive and looked forward to their wedding almost as much as this young couple did. Tim & Denise were working out the arrangements for their wedding - flowers, dress, bridal party and the honeymoon!

One day, during her daily time of prayer, Denise had a unique encounter with God. An angel appeared to her and said she would become pregnant by a miracle of God. Denise was so excited about her encounter that she ran to Tim to share the good news. As Denise enthusiastically shared her experience with Tim, Tim's countenance sank lower and lower.

"Denise, could you just be honest with me? Who is this other guy?"

"There is no one else," she pleaded.

"Denise, please don't talk to me right now. I need some time to pray about this." Tim left as Denise stood alone and dumbfounded.

"God did speak to me, didn't He?" she wondered.

As Tim sought God, he too had a divine encounter and was assured by God that a miracle had taken place.

Then willfully, Tim entered into the shame he knew Denise would carry from being pregnant outside of marriage. Tim & Denise felt alone, misunderstood and embarrassed.

Why would God ask them to walk such a lonely and misunderstood road?

Who would support them? Who would believe in them? What if God asked you to be misunderstood, to have your reputation destroyed or to be maligned according to His will? Would you continue your faith journey or call it quits?

Do you recognize any of these faithful friends above? Put on your seatbelt and consider the following.

Story 1–Job

(Book of Job)

Our "Matt" is really Job. Through no fault of his own, Job was caught in the middle of a cosmic battle. In fact, it wasn't even satan who came up with the idea of afflicting Job. It was God! Imagine, if Job could have eavesdropped on the conversation between God and satan. Job must have wondered what he had done to deserve such a terrible punishment. But it was no punishment. God knew the heart of Job and he used Job to send a message to satan, to those around Job and to you and I thousands of years later.

Think about it–Job lost his children, his business, his health and was deserted by his closest friends in his time of greatest need. They believed his tragedy was due to some secret sin and that a loving God would never do such terrible things to such a righteous man…right?...Wrong! Yet, God used many years of Job's life to accomplish an eternal purpose happening in the heavenly realm. Job was in the middle of a cosmic battle by the very will of God.

Consider that it was God, not satan, who suggested Job be tested. It seems God had enormous confidence in Job. How would you respond if you knew you were caught in a cosmic battle? Could you somehow be more interested in God's glory, in worshipping Him, than in your own suffering? How would you respond differently to your situation if you knew God had the same confidence, right now, in you? He does!

Story 2 – Abraham & Sarah

(Genesis 12-21)

After years of struggling with infertility and the stigma of not having children, Abraham and Sarah (Kwamee & Latisha) were well past their childbearing years. Keep in mind that having many children was viewed as a reflection of God's blessing in the Hebrew culture. They lived with the shame of not having the apparent "blessing of God."

Then God went to Abraham and told him to go to a yet unnamed country. During one evening on a beautiful starry night, you can almost picture God putting His arm around Abraham, looking at the stars with him and promising that He would make Abraham's descendents more numerous than the very stars.

Excited, Abraham almost certainly ran home to Sarah to tell her the good news. Unfortunately, when God promises something, it doesn't always happen on our timetable.

Consider the Israelites before they crossed over into the Promised Land. God said He would "<u>give</u> them the land," yet they had to <u>take</u> it. I imagine that when most of us hear that someone is going to *give* us something, we expect to be eager receivers. Sometimes, as in this case, taking means more than just passively receiving, *taking* means just that, *taking*.

Tens of thousands, perhaps hundreds of thousands of Israelites died in their quest to *take* the land that God said He would *give* them. It took them many years and many lives to *take* the land and realize God's promise.

This happened to be the case with Abraham and Sarah. After weeks and months of trying, nothing happened. Years passed and still no baby. Can you begin to imagine the questions, doubts and frustration that filled their hearts? I wonder what type of support their friends and family gave? Did they support them? Question them? Doubt them? Doubt God? Why would a loving God wait 25 years to fulfill His promise He made to them? Would you wait 25 years to experience the blessing of God? Could you follow hard after God and trust Him in the midst of such silence?

We don't understand all the "whys," but God says that He never forgot His promise, and was fulfilling it according to His eternal timetable.

What if God was working the same way in your life? Could you persevere in faith and patience?

Story 3 – Esther
(Book of Esther)

Our beautiful heroin, "Angie," is Esther. Orphaned and raised by her uncle, Esther had developed a deep and abiding faith in God. Unlike some women, Esther did not use her beauty to manipulate the hearts around her. She was more concerned about turning her heart toward God than turning a guy's head toward her.

The king of her land took Esther for his royal harem. She spent a year in training and she excelled in all her "duties" to the extent that she earned the favor of the king and eventually became queen. During her time as queen, she learned of a plot to destroy the Jewish race. After consulting her uncle and taking several days to fast and pray, she risked her life by approaching the king without being summoned.

One would think, "Hasn't she been through enough?" Esther lost her dreams, was used as a sex object and now is being called upon to risk her life. She will never know the exclusive love of one man. What's the deal God?

Through her heroism and faith, she saved her people from genocide. Why did God allow the events of Esther's life to occur? He used these events to place Esther in just the right place, at just the right time to save an entire nation!

But why didn't God just share the deal up front? Why didn't He tell her of His great plan? God never says why. In fact, He's never explicitly mentioned in the entire book. The implication is that He is in the background overseeing her journey. He does seem to have a great confidence in her heart and in her faith.

Most people would have understood if she were angry, bitter, resentful, or had even given up on God. What kind of God would allow this type of pain in a person's life? How much can we really expect one person to bear? Her entire future was changed in a moment at the hands of a selfish king under the will of God.

Yet, she alone was in the perfect place, at the perfect time, to accomplish God's perfect plan. Her whole life seems to have been built up for this vital moment.

What if God were preparing you for some great place in His eternal plan? What if God was raising you up for "such a time as this?" What price would you pay to be used by God to accomplish His purpose?

Story 4 – Joseph
(Genesis 37-50)

Joseph (Kyle) was the youngest in his family. In the Hebrew culture, the oldest was the next patriarch of the family and received a double portion of the inheritance. Not a whole lot was expected from the youngest, let alone one that was a bit on the arrogant side.

Nonetheless, God spoke to Joseph in a dream. In his excitement Joseph shared His dream with his family only to have them feel his arrogance had gone a bit too far this time. One day while Joseph was seeking to serve his brothers, they finally lost patience. They wanted him dead! Now that's upset! After being thrown into a pit by his brothers, his life was spared, only through the insistence of his oldest brother and he was sold into slavery instead of being killed.

Imagine looking up from the bottom of that pit, listening to the arguments debating whether he would be killed or sold. Imagine the shock, bewilderment, betrayal and confusion he felt as he was shackled and led away, watching as his brothers joyfully and excitedly divided the money amongst themselves.

Still, Joseph loved God and God prospered him. He was sold to Potiphar, an Egyptian leader, and God prospered Joseph who prospered Potiphar. Potiphar's trust in Joseph grew.

As time went by, Potiphar traveled much and his wife became lonely and was looking for companionship while her husband was on the road.

Potiphar's wife made several advances toward Joseph, but Joseph remained faithful to God and his master. Finally, one day when the house was unusually quiet and the servants were not around, Mrs. Potiphar made one last desperate move to have Joseph. She actually grabbed him. Joseph ran and she ended up with just his tunic in her hand. Scorned and embarrassed, she cried rape.

Potiphar came home to hear his wife's cries and confronted Joseph. Under normal circumstances, Joseph should have been killed, yet, it seems Potiphar knew not just Joseph, but he also knew his wife. To save face, he threw Joseph in prison. Joseph is even forgotten by his friend whom he helped so much in prison. Finally, years later Joseph is called to interpret a dream for the king.

The king is so impressed that he makes Joseph second in command over the entire nation. From there, God used Joseph to save a nation, including his own family, from famine.

Imagine, over 13 years of life wasted away in prison for sharing a God-given vision. Imagine the hurt, anguish, betrayal and confusion Joseph must have felt. Somewhere down the line, Joseph trusted his life and future to the God who made the promise to him.

These years of struggle changed him. Years later, when he reunited with his brothers, even though he had the power to have them executed on the spot, his heart of compassion overwhelmed him and he wept out of his deep love for them. "...you meant evil against me, but God meant it for good..." (Genesis 50:20).

Could you say that about your circumstances of life? Could you serve God faithfully for over 13 years if you had been betrayed, abandoned, misunderstood and falsely imprisoned? Could you trust in God's sovereignty over your life - no matter what? Even if it takes a lifetime? Joseph did!

Joseph didn't know what God was going to do, but he trusted God in spite of his circumstances. He believed God was true and faithful, despite his situation.

Story 5 – David
(1 Samuel 15-2 Samuel 2)

One day while David, our "Ed," was caring for his father's sheep, a prophet of God, Samuel, came to his house in search of the nation's next king. This day would forever change his life because he was then anointed to be the future king of Israel.

Later in David's life, he overheard Goliath, a giant, and enemy to David's people challenge the fleeing soldiers of Israel. David was moved by his love for God and through his trust in God, he killed Goliath. After his victory, the people gave more praise to David than the present king, King Saul, liked. Saul became jealous and desired to kill David. For the next 15 years, David spent his life running from Saul. Even though David could have killed Saul on two occasions, he entrusted his future and Saul's life to the God he continued to love and follow.

Eventually, David became king and God used him to unite the divided nation of Israel. David did not seek or specifically train to be king. God selected him in His divine plan because David was obedient and faithful in his ordinary daily responsibilities.

Through his life, David had to overcome the misunderstanding, injustice, upheaval and confusion that came from following God.

Story 6 – Mary & Joseph

(Matthew 1, Luke 1:26-2:40)

According to the Law of the Old Testament, adultery or immorality was punishable by death. Even Jesus, did not seek to deplore the capital punishment of the woman caught in adultery (He affirmed it), but He deplored the hypocrisy among her accusers. When the angel appeared to Mary and shared the good news of her upcoming pregnancy, Mary was literally being asked to place her life at risk to obey God.

Since Joseph confirmed he was not the father, the earthly perspective from friends and family was that she had been immoral with another man. Look at her situation from a parent's perspective. If your daughter came home excited about her devotional time with God and shared that God had spoken to her, I imagine as a godly parent you'd share her excitement. But what if she shared she was expecting a baby by the "power of God." I imagine you'd have more than a few questions for her and when it was all said and done, her "God did it" story might not be enough.

God was asking Mary to risk her life, her reputation and her future to obey Him. She would have to spend a good part of her life living with the shame of being perceived as an immoral woman. Some may have even thought of Jesus as the bastard of the family. I imagine for some, that mere thought is heresy. Yet, from the community's perspective, would this not be true?

Consider Joseph. God asked him to enter into Mary's shame. Some may even have thought him to be a liar about their apparent sexual indiscretion, since he continued to take Mary as his wife and didn't break off the engagement. Imagine the talk in the town as people saw them walking down the street holding hands with Mary's tummy bulging.

Yet as a result of their obedience, Mary brought forth the Savior of the World, the very Savior that has touched and changed your life. Joseph got to raise God's own Son. Jesus was Joseph's "step child," yet Joseph regarded Him as his own son.

Would you enter into such shame and misunderstanding? Would you still follow God in spite the rejection and scorn of others?

Encountering the Darkness

Now faith is the assurance of things hoped for,
the conviction of things not seen.
Hebrews 11:1

You may be wondering why so many stories are listed here. If you're like me, I don't want someone to take a few isolated examples and over-generalize. It is important to understand that God's work is characterized by such wildness and goodness. There are many more stories that could be listed here as well (Consider Moses, Noah, Hannah, Jonathan, Uriah, Gideon, Samuel, Jeremiah, Paul, Peter, Jonah, Stephen, Epaphroditus, Amos, Daniel, Debra, etc.).

The Bible is filled with many other stories of men and women who endured much pain, lost their lives and experienced misfortune as a result of following God. Hebrews chapter 11 is the "hall of fame" of faith. This is the road of suffering to which God called them and to which He calls us.

By definition (Hebrews 11:1), "faith is the assurance of things hoped for, the conviction of things not seen." Isn't this what walking in the darkness is all about...faith? Faith is walking where we cannot see the outcome. Faith is learning to walk in the darkness. Faith is learning to trust God when circumstances appear to indicate otherwise.

Faith is so critical that a few verses later, Hebrews 11:6 (NIV) says "that without faith it is impossible to please Him, for he who comes to God must believe that He is, and that He is a rewarder of those that seek Him." There is something about faith that touches and turns the heart of God. Without faith, it is absolutely impossible to please God.

Galatians 5:6 (NIV) states that all that matters is "faith expressing itself in love." God is moved by faith and He wants you and I to be men and women of faith, men and women who walk through the darkness by faith. I would urge you to consider the challenges these people faced.

Consider the Great Apostle Paul. 2 Corinthians 6:3-13 & 11:16-33 (NIV) share the struggles he endured in his obedience to God.

> Chapter 6 "We put no stumbling block in anyone's path, so that our ministry will not be discredited. Rather, as servants of God we commend ourselves in every way; in great endurance; in troubles, hardships and distresses; in beatings, imprisonments and riots; in hard work, sleepless nights and hunger; in purity, understanding, patience and kindness; in the Holy Spirit and in sincere love; in truthful speech and

in the power of God; with weapons of righteousness in the right hand and in the left; through glory and dishonor, bad report and good report; genuine, yet regarded as impostors; known, yet regarded as unknown; dying, and yet we live on; beaten, and yet not killed; sorrowful, yet always rejoicing; poor, yet making many rich; having nothing, and yet possessing everything.

We have spoken freely to you, Corinthians, and opened wide our hearts to you. We are not withholding our affection from you, but you are withholding yours from us. As a fair exchange-I speak as to my children-open wide your hearts also."

Chapter 11 "I repeat; Let no one take me for a fool. But if you do, then receive me just as you would a fool, so that I may do a little boasting. In this self-confident boasting I am not talking as the Lord would, but as a fool. Since many are boasting in the way the world does, I too will boast. You gladly put up with fools since you are so wise! In fact, you even put up with anyone who enslaves you or exploits you or takes advantage of you or pushes himself forward or slaps you in the face. To my shame I admit that we were too weak for that!

What anyone else dares to boast about
– I am speaking as a fool – I also dare to
boast about. Are they Hebrews? So am
I. Are they Israelites? So am I. Are they
Abraham's descendents? So am I. Are
they servants of Christ? (I am out of my
mind to talk like this.) I am more. I have
worked much harder, been in prison more
frequently, been flogged more severely,
and been exposed to death again and
again. Five times I received from the Jews
the forty lashes minus one. Three times I
was beaten with rods, once I was stoned,
three times I was shipwrecked, I spent a
night and a day in the open sea. I have been
constantly on the move. I have been in
danger from rivers, in danger from bandits,
in danger from my own countrymen, in
danger from Gentiles, in danger in the city,
in danger in the country, in danger at sea;
and in danger from false brothers. I have
labored and toiled and have often gone
without sleep; I have known hunger and
thirst and have often gone without food; I
have been cold and naked. Besides everything else, I face daily the pressure of my
concern for all the churches. Who is weak,
and I do not feel weak? Who is led into sin,
and I do not inwardly burn?

If I must boast, I will boast of the things
that show my weakness. The God and

Father of the Lord Jesus, who is to be praised forever, knows that I am not lying. In Damascus the governor under King Aretas had the city of Damascus guarded in order to arrest me. But I was lowered in a basket from a window in the wall and slipped through his hands."

Not only are these struggles listed, but you're also told that all of Asia deserted him (2 Timothy 1:15). You're told of Alexander the coppersmith that he "did me much harm" (2 Timothy 4:14). In Corinth, because of those improperly peddling the Gospel for profit, Paul labored night and day as a tentmaker to offer the Gospel for free to avoid this accusation. Paul knew pain.

Even God knows pain. He lost a third of Heaven from the betrayal and fall of satan. Imagine God's broken heart with the fall of Adam & Eve. Imagine the grieving heart of God that would cause Him to destroy His creation except for eight people with a flood. Imagine God's despair as He was separated from His Son, Jesus, for the first time in eternity as Jesus hung on the cross. Consider God's grieving heart as He watched men and women throughout history abuse their God-given freedom to take advantage of and harm others for their own greed and selfishness.

I don't know what pain you've experienced in your life. I imagine, if you're like most people, you've had some terrible things happen to you. I would challenge you to wrestle with God...and lose. Surrender to Him. If you win, you lose, since you get your own way without God. If you lose, you win, since God's will is best!

I have made a regular habit in my life to get extended times away with God over the years...a sort of "vacation with God." During these times, I avoid TV, cell phones, internet and other people in order to get quiet before God. God says to "be still, and know that I am God" (Psalm 46:10 NIV).

Several years ago, as I was grappling with some of the injustices and inequities of my life, I decided to let God have it. I shared my frustration and disappointment at His lack of involvement. I shared my anger with Him for allowing evil to triumph even though I sought to love God with all my heart and made great sacrifices for the cause of Christ. I had been afraid to share those ideas with Him or verbalize them. Yet, I became convicted that God already knew what was in my heart, yet I was not being "real" with God or myself. I was pretending that if I didn't share my disappointments, and only thought them, somehow God didn't know. The only person I was fooling was myself.

During one of my "vacations with God," I made a list of my challenges. I began to share my deepest disappointments with Him. I sought Him with tears for understanding and clarity.

"God, I'm tired of feeling alone. I'm sick and tired of feeling misunderstood. I'm tired of being slandered. God, I feel like I've given my best and it's not good enough. It seems that those around me feel that their problems are my fault. I feel like I'm the one left holding the bag. In my times of pain it seems that I need to help those closest to me to help me. I feel I've been betrayed and abandoned by those around me. God, I'm not in control the way I want to be and I feel lost, I feel alone, I feel powerless, as if my world is spinning out of control. God, please help and guide me! Otherwise, I'm afraid I'm not going to make it. God, if you're the loving, powerful, ever present God you say that you are, please help me to understand, even a little, how the tragedies in my life demonstrate Your goodness."

As I opened myself up, God began to reveal how the hurts, disappointments and inequities of my life had made me more like Jesus. God had used those times to make me more patient; He made me stronger emotionally; He made me more secure; He made me more of a man of faith; He made me more in love with Him. It started to make sense…a little…enough to give me hope and re-energize my heart.

Ultimately, God's plan for my life and for yours is to conform us to the image of Jesus (Romans 8:29). God, knowing us, His creation, often uses adversity to shape our lives and hearts. If you doubt that, just read your Bible. It's full of stories of how God takes people into circumstances that they would never have chosen on their own in order to make them a people conformed to His image. The same is true for you.

I began to thank Jesus for my pain. Seeing a glimpse of what He had done in my life, I told Him that I would do it all over again to become the new person that I now am today and the hope of the person I will become in the future. Imagine that. I was telling Jesus I would willfully choose to go through the abandonment and abuse all over again to become the man I am today!

Perhaps Romans 8:28 was true after all, "... that God causes all things to work together for good to those who love God, to those who are called according to His purpose."

I was reminded of a quote that says, "God wounds deeply those that He uses greatly." Perhaps God was preparing me for some future ministry yet to be revealed.

The other realization that brought me to tears was the intimacy I experienced with Jesus during this time. Although I had greatly hated and despised the pain and circumstances that I went through, I greatly loved this special closeness with Jesus. He allowed me to experience His love in a special way in the midst of my painful circumstances. It was the ultimate love-hate relationship. I hated what I had gone through, yet I loved the intimacy that this pain allowed with Jesus. I concluded I would rather spend my life with the challenges than lose this intimacy with Jesus that I had obtained in the midst of the pain.

Wow! What a place to be. It seems that the greater the pain and suffering, the greater the nearness and the intimacy of God. I said like Jesus at Gethsemane, "... not my will, but Yours be done" (Luke 22:42 NIV).

Consider Jesus' Garden of Gethsemane experience. He is God. He knows what's coming and every detail of what will happen regarding His crucifixion. He was about to be betrayed by a man with whom he had spent years. He knew the men that He, God, had been disciplining and loving for over the last three and a half years would desert Him in His very moment of need. He's so stressed over His upcoming torture and death, that the capillaries in His face are bursting and He's sweating drops of blood.

I don't know anyone who's been that stressed, but Jesus was. And Jesus was completely innocent in every way and thought imaginable. You and I can't say that! Yet, He came to a place where He said, "not My will but Yours be done."

Could you say that? Could you give yourself to the wildness and unpredictability of God? Could you walk in such darkness? C.S. Lewis in the "Chronicles of Narnia," said that "God is not safe, but He is good." For some, this statement is worth meditating on before you dismiss it. God is good, yet as we've just considered, He's called His faithful followers to some very unsafe and unnerving steps of obedience, risking even their very lives, vocations, fortunes and futures.

If you do not look at your circumstances through the lens of all loving, all caring, all powerful, all knowing, ever present Creator God, then you will most likely come to the conclusion in your anger and bitterness that God is a liar. You may conclude He did not do what He said and therefore He cannot be trusted, He is not worth following and maybe He ultimately does not even exist.

Jesus commanded you are to take up your cross daily and follow Him (Luke 9:23). Carrying your cross is to stumble your way toward death. Perhaps figuratively, perhaps literally, you do not know, but carry your cross you must.

Jesus also told you to walk the narrow road (Matthew 7:13-14), the road less traveled as told by S. Peck. One secret of the narrow road is that the farther you go, the lonelier it becomes. Fewer and fewer people are willing to pay the cost of walking the road less traveled. There is something unique about the loneliness of being on the narrow road and the special intimacy with Jesus that it brings.

Another secret of the narrow road is that it gets narrower the further you go. Sometimes the road is so narrow that you feel your shoulders rubbing against its sides and feel it's impossible to go any further. Then at just the right moment, when you think you can go no further, Jesus makes a way.

The Apostle Paul in Colossians 1:24 shares how he completed the sufferings of Christ. I wrestled with this passage for years. Didn't Jesus die for all on the cross? Wasn't His atonement for us complete? What could Paul do that Jesus couldn't or wouldn't do?

I think I now have a glimpse of what he meant. I believe Paul was talking about "redemptive suffering." Jesus did die for all the sins for all the people that have been, are and ever will be. But you and I suffer and are hurt as we seek to take this wonderful message of hope to a fallen and lost world.

Ministry can be abusive. Fighting for the hearts and souls of people is ugly front-line work. To stand in the gap is to put yourself in harm's way. If the people you minister to were angry with their parents, they will most likely be angry with you. If people in authority who should have protected them have abused them, they will most likely be suspicious and doubtful of you. Since most people have never experienced unconditional love, gestures of kindness will most likely be viewed with suspicion and doubt.

I could go on, but you get the idea. You are in the middle of a cosmic battle fighting for the eternal souls of others. In 2 Timothy 3:12 (NIV), the Apostle Paul shares that "...all who desire to live godly in Christ Jesus will be persecuted." Just to <u>desire</u> to live godly puts you in the cross hairs of the devil, how much more so if you're actively living out your faith.

You will experience unjust suffering, redemptive suffering, as you live, as you love and as you serve. This redemptive suffering may be from those with whom you seek to share the good news. Your redemptive suffering may be the result of being in the wrong place at the wrong time through no fault of your own. Your redemptive suffering may be the result of helping another in their faith journey as they wrestle with and work through issues in their life. Yet God in His infinite wisdom has allowed this redemptive suffering in your life to display His glory.

I don't claim to understand all of this, but I do know this: If God did what He did to some of His faithful followers you read about in your Bible, then He surely could do the same with me and with you.

Perhaps I'm caught in a cosmic battle. Perhaps God is doing something special He will share with me at some future date. Perhaps God is preparing me for some awesome future ministry. Perhaps God is using me for the sake of another. Perhaps He is using this situation to reveal a unique aspect of Himself to me or perhaps He is refining me to be made more in His likeness. Whatever the case, God is good and although suffering is yucky, what it produces will conform me more and more to the image of Jesus, if I respond in faith and trust by the power of His Spirit. There is value in suffering.

I'm not an artistic person, yet I have had images in my mind I have wanted to express, but have had no way to do so. They have been trapped within me. I asked God to give me a simple way that a non-artist like me could express some thoughts and emotions I've experienced through a basic art medium. What follows is an answer to that prayer.

Hopelessness

Hope deferred makes the heart sick.
Proverbs 13:12

This simple picture represents the despair, hopelessness, darkness and uncertainty I faced in my darkest hours of wrestling with my disappointment with God. Take a moment and imagine yourself surrounded by this blackness. It was so dark I could not see my hand in front of my face. It was so heavy I felt I couldn't move. It was so silent that even as I spoke, the words seemed to vanish. I felt so alone and so lost. I felt like my world was collapsing upon me and I was so paralyzed by fear that I was afraid to move, and I didn't feel like I could move even if I wanted. I despaired even of life and I was looking for a way out...out of life. The weight of it all was crushing. Have you ever felt this way?

Hope

Now may the God of hope
fill you with all joy and peace in believing,
so that you will abound in hope
by the power of the Holy Spirit.
Romans 15:13

Somewhere on the journey, a tiny, very tiny pinpoint of light manifested itself in the far distance. I call this hope. It was my breakthrough! Imagine once again being surrounded by the darkness and seeing this tiny pinpoint of light. Romans 15:13 says "Now may the God of Hope fill you with all joy and peace in believing, that you will abound in hope by the power of the Holy Spirit."

God is a God of hope and He wants you to abound in hope by the power of His Holy Spirit. I didn't believe that God was a God of hope and this verse and picture changed my life. It really didn't matter how far away the light was. I knew that if I kept walking one small step at a time, it would get bigger and bigger and I was determined to keep walking no matter how long it took. No matter what the cost. I wanted healing. As I walked, it got bigger and my hope and my heart grew too, till eventually came....

Peace

"Peace I leave with you;
My peace I give to you."
John 14:27

Peace is a place of rest and light-heartedness. The darkness is no longer in sight. The crushing weight is lifted. I am surrounded by light and peace. The odd thing about the peace of Christ is that it can be experienced in the very midst of the hardship and suffering. I can face my circumstances without fear because of the nearness of God. "Be anxious for nothing, but in prayer and supplication with thanksgiving let your requests be made known to God. And the peace of God, which surpasses all comprehension, shall guard your hearts and your minds in Christ Jesus" (Philippians. 4:6-7).

Experiencing the Light

"I am the Light of the world;
he who follows Me will not walk in the darkness,
but will have the Light of life."
John 8:12

I don't know what you now face. I don't know what terrible things have happened in your life; yet I, like you, know pain. I know uncertainty, I know doubt and I know despair. I know betrayal and I know abandonment. I also now know at some level the love of God.

As I struggled in my journey, I sensed God speaking three things to me that helped me keep walking through the darkness:

1) God was pleased with me.

> What happened to me was not a result of some secret sin of mine, but it was the harsh reality of living in a fallen world where people sometimes use their "freedom" at the expense of others.

I didn't deserve these bad things, yet God permitted them to happen. He loved me and was pleased with me no matter what, even if I had messed up. He was using what may have been meant for evil to conform me to His image.

2) God asked me to walk in the darkness.

God said there were no guarantees regarding the outcome of my circumstances. He told me to walk in the darkness. One step at a time, facing my fears and my insecurities in the midst of my helplessness, my powerlessness and my hopelessness, God asked me to walk in the darkness, yet I felt alone.

3) God was with me.

It's interesting that God said He was with me. He understood that I felt alone. It's also interesting that all throughout the Bible, God has continually reminded His followers that He was with them. This gave me such a great hope knowing that I was not alone, that I did not need to be afraid, that I would not stumble in the darkness and even if I did, God would be there.

I hope you will reflect and meditate upon these pictures. I hope these pictures and these thoughts can mean even more to you than they have for me. They have greatly shaped and changed my life. I don't want to give you the impression that I have arrived and that am perfect, for no one on this side of eternity is. I still have enormous doubts and enormous insecurities with which I grapple. Yet, God has revealed a bit of Himself to me through my pain and I wait with eager expectation for what He may yet reveal.

Experiencing God in my pain has been one of the most powerful experiences of my life. I believe I've encountered God. He has enabled me to persevere when I should have crumbled under the weight and pressure. God wants to do the same and even more for you!

One final note, God doesn't waste a hurt. You live in a broken, hopeless, helpless and fallen world. People are silently and not so silently agonizing over the pain in their life. Who will help them? Who will offer them hope? The Apostle Paul shares that you can comfort others with the comfort God has given you (2 Corinthians 1:3-7).

You don't even have to figure it all out. God regularly uses "wounded soldiers" who've experienced at some level His peace and His grace so that they can give it away to others even while they're still in the midst of the battle. God wants you to minister His grace to others even as you fight your fight of faith. If you wait till it's all worked out, you may never share this wonderful message of hope to others since you'll never be whole or pain-free here on earth. I can assure you, even as I write this, I don't have all of my issues figured out.

Your experiences can provide hope to the hopeless, healing to the broken-hearted and light in the midst of the darkness for others. Knowing that you're not alone and that circumstances can get better is often enough to encourage those who are struggling and is often a great encouragement to others who wrestle with similar issues as well. You and I may be the only "Jesus" some people will ever meet.

My hope and prayer for you is that you will take your burdens to God, that you will ask Him to reveal Himself in light of His Truth to help you understand how He wants to use your situations to conform you more and more to His image for His glory. I pray that His nearness and intimacy will forever change your life and heart and that you will know Him more deeply. I pray that you will walk in courage and in faith. I pray that you will move from being a victim to being a victor and from tragedy to triumph. May His love and peace rest upon you to experience the abundant life He's called you to as you walk through the darkness.

Encountering God

In order to walk through the darkness and encounter the light, you must encounter God. As you surrender your life to Jesus, God promises to give you His Spirit to empower, to guide and to strengthen you to do His will.

Experiencing God is as easy as ABC, in reverse order.

Confess
> *"For all have sinned and fall short of the glory of God." Romans 3:23*

Let's be honest, no one is perfect. Everyone makes mistakes either intentionally or unintentionally. The biblical word for mistakes is sin. The word "sin" literally means "to miss the mark" and in context, it means to miss God's perfect standard. In fact, your mistakes create a separation between you and God (Isaiah 59:2). Sin makes it impossible for you to connect with God because a perfect God cannot connect with the imperfect people even though God deeply loves everyone, including you. A relationship to encounter God begins with confessing that you are not perfect and are separated from a relationship with God. Confession is just the first step, you must also believe.

Believe

> *"For God so loved the world, that He gave His only begotten Son, that whoever believes in Him shall not perish, but have eternal life." John 3:16*

At Christmas, the world celebrates the birth of Jesus Christ. Not just the birth of a man, but God birthed in human form. Jesus lived a perfect life. Unlike us, He never made a mistake. He was crucified on a cross as a sacrifice for the mistakes of all mankind. Yet the most important event in human history was not the death of Jesus, it was that fact that Jesus Christ resurrected from the dead. His resurrection proved that He is God and that the payment He made to forgive you of your mistakes was acceptable to God the Father.

Jesus Christ is the bridge between God and mankind. His death and resurrection provides a way for every person to experience forgiveness and redemption and to enter into a personal relationship with God. To experience this relationship with Jesus, you must accept His free gift of forgiveness.

Accept

> *"For the wages of sin is death, but the free gift of God is eternal life in Christ Jesus our Lord." Romans 6:23*

The Bible describes a relationship with God as a free gift. Like a gift, you cannot earn it. You cannot buy it. You cannot be religious enough. You do not even deserve it. You must humbly accept it. Encountering God is as simple as asking. As you admit your imperfection, as you believe that you are forgiven through the sacrificial death of Jesus, as you place your hope in the resurrection of Jesus from the dead, you simply surrender leadership of your life to Him. Invite Jesus into your heart. This simple act of surrender transforms you and the Spirit of God enters your heart the moment you believe. God's Spirit gives you the power, understanding and guidance to do all that God asks you to do.

Here is a sample prayer that you could pray to surrender your life to Jesus.

Dear Jesus,

> *I confess that I have done wrong. I believe that You are God and that You died to forgive me for my sins. Thank You for dying for me and proving this hope through Your resurrection from the dead. I accept this amazing gift and I surrender myself to You. I invite You into my life. As You have died for me, I want to live for You. Thank You for accepting me and thank You for empowering me to live in a way that will glorify You. Amen*

If you prayed this prayer, congratulations and welcome into the family of Jesus. This is the most important decision you will ever make on earth because it determines your eternal destiny. You may not feel different or look different. Yet over the next weeks and months, you may notice differences in your thoughts and actions that reflect that the Spirit of God is working in and through you.

It is the Spirit of God that will enable you to be all that Jesus wants you to be so that you can more effectively know and grow into Christ-likeness.

If you surrendered your life to Jesus, contact me at Jeff@MCFcc.org and I will forward you some resources to help you get started in this exciting new life with Jesus.

Health Considerations

It is important to understand that significant issues that affect your life, whether one time occurrences or events that have taken place over years, may and can lead to depression even serious depression. Often as you fight the fight of faith, you are clinically depressed.

Although I am not a doctor, there are several factors that have influenced me and others to be in the best position to deal with these difficult issues of the heart. Be sure to consult with your doctor before making changes to your lifestyle.

Sleep

We are a sleep-deprived nation. If you are not getting 7-9 hours of sleep, your body and mind may not be getting enough time to repair and refresh itself. Be sure to get adequate and appropriate rest.

On the other hand, if you're regularly getting more than 10 hours of sleep, you may be dealing with a depression that requires the advice and counsel of a qualified Christian professional (Medical Doctor, Psychologist, Psychiatrist, Counselor, etc.).

Refreshment

Having your body, mind and soul refreshed is vitally important. Taking an inventory of your life and re-evaluating priorities is essential. Identifying people and activities that refresh you and those that are draining to you is very important. This evaluation should be done on a relational as well as on a task level. Making more time to get with people who refresh you and doing those tasks that bring refreshment is vitally important.

It is important to note that you may not be able to avoid some tasks and some people that are more draining to you due to your commitments and/or obligations. In those cases, setting appropriate boundaries on those tasks and relationships can minimize the draining component.

It is also important to evaluate your spiritual life. What practices bring you the greatest refreshment? How much of a priority do you make those activities? Waiting for the right time to do them may seldom happen...make the time. Your "to-do" list will still be there and it can wait.

Exercise

The benefits of exercise are well documented. Even 20 minutes of moderate exercise just 3 times a week can make a big difference.

Diet

Be sure to eat a well-balanced diet. Your body needs proper nutrition to function well. A poor diet may affect your physiological and psychological well-being. Taking depressants, such as alcohol, while struggling with depression may make your depression deeper and more difficult to control.

Medication

Many people of faith have negative attitudes regarding the use of psychological medication to fight depression. It has been my experience in working with many people that the use of medication brings a balance that "levels the playing field" in order to deal with these deep issues of the heart.

If you choose to use medication, be patient. It is not uncommon for it to take 4-18 months to find the right medication that brings balance, with side effects that you can live with.

Also, if you take medications and start to feel better, don't quit taking them. Be sure to consult with your doctor since some of these medications must be discontinued in a systematic manner.

Counselor

A qualified Christian counselor can make a world of difference. A counselor who shares your faith and understands the physiological and psychological factors can facilitate a God encounter that brings healing and freedom. A counselor is not a quick fix. It may take years to unpack and process the challenges you have faced. Please be patient.

To maximize the counseling process, I recommend signing a waiver to allow your pastor, small group leader or close friend to discuss your situation with your counselor. Having others interact with your counselor, allows the counselor to get a greater understanding of all facets of your situation in order to best serve and minister to you. Counseling can be a great support until God visits you in your place of need.

Support Group

God wants you connected to others, that is why Jesus established the church. In addition, the psychological field has documented that a good small group or support group can be more effective than a good counselor. Why? Your counselor sees you for about an hour per week and only gets your perspective regarding your situation. Your small group may see you multiple times per week and can add a different perspective to your life experiences. Do not underestimate the importance or value of being connected in a loving small group community.

A supportive small group where you can feel safe, be supported and be held accountable in achieving your goals is paramount. Whether your support group is in or out of your church family, trust God to provide this team to help you and then support one another to help achieve wholeness in each other's walk through the darkness.

About Jeff

Jeff is the founding and senior pastor of MCF Community Church. He is nearing the end of raising four children and shares from over 20 years of personal child-raising experience and over 30 years of ministry experience.

As a college student at The Ohio State University, he surrendered his life to Jesus in 1982. He graduated with a BS in Electrical Engineering and worked for American Electric Power after graduation until he left to plant a church in Kent, Ohio. While in Kent, he worked for the Hoover Company as a design engineer before leaving to attend Kent State for his Master of Business Administration. He met Dawn, his wife, at Kent State and after their marriage, they moved to the Maryland after their graduations to work with the student ministry at the University of Maryland. Jesus has done an amazing work in and through his life and ministry. Being teamed up with the people of MCF, has been an honor and a privilege.

Jeff and Dawn were married in 1989 and now live in Greenbelt, Maryland. They have four children, Jimmy, Danny, Katie, and Johnny.

While serving the ministry at the University of Maryland, Jeff actually accepted a full-time ministry position for part-time pay (yes, he was a little crazy)! To be totally honest, there is bad news and good news. The bad news is that he grew the campus ministry from 40 to 8 in his first few years at the University of Maryland (yes, it was a rough start). The good news is that God is greater and the ministry has grown from those 8 brave souls to the vibrant ministry it is today! After 23 years of campus ministry at the University of Maryland, MCF Community Church launched June 5, 2011. Jeff hopes you'll be an active change agent for the Kingdom of God and go to the next level and impact more people to know and grow in Jesus!

Jeff loves to run and is a triathlete. Currently, he has completed 7 marathons (Oct 2011-under 5 hours!-not bad for an older guy) and has completed several sprint triathlons, half-Ironman and a full Ironman! He has his eyes on more marathons in the future! So yes, he is a type "A" personality and a recovering perfectionist.

Life Scriptures
Jeff lives to hear the words...
"Well done good and faithful Servant"
Matthew 25:21 NIV

"Let all you do be done in Love"
1 Corinthians 16:14 NIV

Jeff has also prepared a number of materials to help others in their faith in Christ. Many are found under the **Resources** page at **www.MCFcc.org** and are listed below.

Other Resources by Jeff Warner

Books

Walking Through the Darkness
Discover why an all-loving, all-powerful God allows bad things to happen to good people. There is meaning in suffering!

Dating Successfully
Explore Biblical principles to developing godly relationships and finding the love of your life.

My First Steps in Faith
New to the Christian faith? This book will help introduce you to your new life in Christ.

Proverbs: The Book of Wisdom (Topical Format)
The book of Proverbs organized by topic.

God's Promises
Key Bible verses organized by topic.

e-Books & Booklets

The Picture That Changed My Life

A provocative, interactive and simple way to share your faith in Christ.

Tithing: An Issue of the Heart

Encounter God's heart to bless your life to the fullest through your financial stewardship.

Raising Happy & Obedient Children

Apply God's truth to raising children who are able to obey quickly, sit quietly and are a powerful witness of God's amazing love.

Wealth Builder

Tired of running out of money before the month is out? Learn time-tested principles of Biblical money management and how to maximize your wealth!

My Next Steps Bible Study Series

Next Steps are crucial to growing your faith.
This series will help empower you to live out
God's purposes for your life.

My Next Steps Toward Membership
(2 Week Bible Study)
Daily Bible study to discover the importance of church membership.

My Next Steps Toward Maturity: The Holy Spirit
(1 Week Bible Study)
Daily Bible study to discover and understand the role of the Holy Spirit in your life.

My Next Steps Toward Maturity
(4 Week Bible Study)
Daily Bible study to discover practices essential to spiritual growth.

My Next Steps Toward Ministry
(2 Week Bible Study)
Daily Bible study to discover your unique service to the body of Christ.

My Next Steps Toward Mission
(2 Week Bible Study)
Daily Bible study to discover your life-long mission serving Jesus.

Audio Messages

Jeff's Messages – Audio Archives
www.MCFcc.org/teachings

Bible Reading Plans

Bible Reading Plans (Semester Based)
www.MCFcc.org/resources

Daily Word of Encouragement
A daily Bible devotion buffet. Each day you'll receive a reading from the New Testament, Old Testament, *Purpose Driven Life* by Rick Warren and *My Utmost for His Highest* by Oswald Chambers. Choose one or two areas, read along, obey and watch your life transform.

Come Be Our Guest At
MCF Community Church

MCF is a non-denominational church
serving the DC Metro area.
We are excited to provide
a culturally relevant and practical church.
We're all about experiencing God in all of His
Grace.

Come checkout the experience!

Our mission is to be a missional,
Christ-centered community.
We seek to communicate the love of Jesus
in words and deeds.

Whether you're an inquisitive seeker
or a long-time believer,
MCF is a safe place to explore and grow your faith.

More info at:
www.MCFcc.org

Notes

Notes

Notes

1888-222 9688

CPSIA information can be obtained at www.ICGtesting.com
Printed in the USA
BVOW03s0431180814

363091BV00001B/1/P

9 781600 343605